Charlotte Moss
A Flair For Living

Other books by Charlotte Moss:

A Passion for Detail (1991)
Creating A Room (1995)
The Poetry of Home (1998)
Design Inspirations, Vol I (2004)
Winter House (2005)

For more information on Charlotte Moss,
or to visit The Townhouse website, please go to www.charlottemoss.com

Text and photographs © Charlotte Moss
www.charlottemoss.com

© 2008 Assouline Publishing
601 West 26th Street, 18th floor
New York, NY 10001, USA
Tel.: 212 989-6810   Fax: 212 647-0005
www.assouline.com

Color separation by Luc Alexis Chasleries

Printed in China

ISBN: 978 2 75940 265 6

Photography by Pieter Estersohn

Charlotte Moss
A Flair For Living

ASSOULINE

Charlotte Moss
A Flair For Living

Preface

Let's start with this: Living is a luxury. If you accept that premise, as I do, you have acknowledged two things. First, that my being here today, writing this right now on a gorgeous day, sitting in my garden in New York City with my dogs at my feet, and now you reading it—well, that is a luxury too. Second, that you share my definition of luxury in its simplest form: breathing.

I remind myself all the time how lucky I am to have grown into this wonderful profession of interior design. The great privilege of wandering, searching, thinking, reading, traveling, meeting with expert craftspeople, artists, fabric manufacturers, upholsterers, wallpaper specialists, carpetmakers, silversmiths, and antiques dealers, and decorating—to be able to do all this and call it work. What a boring, inadequate word to describe all of this.

My work is my joy. I get excited turning the pages of a new auction catalog or receiving a phone call from an antiques dealer informing me of a new shipment. Doing research in the library of a museum or viewing an exhibition with an audio guide is like being transported to an artist's studio, a tapestry factory, or the atelier of a remarkable *ébéniste*.

We are all that we have seen, what we're looking at now, and what will catch our eye next. Wherever we go, we look, we stare, we linger. We catch tantalizing glimpses of places, objects, people. We accumulate images; we store; we assimilate. In a way, we absorb all of these things. They enrich our lives, suffusing our beings. They inform our decisions; they delight our senses; and they expand our memory.

While travel is one of the greatest teachers and a wonderful source of inspiration, reading—often called armchair travel—also has a transporting capacity, essential for all romantics. When looking through a book of beautiful paintings, how many times have you felt as if you were actually floating along a Venetian canal under a Turner sky, or felt the warmth of the sun beaming down on you as you strolled among the sunflowers in Saint-Rémy-de-Provence, or felt the chill on your cheeks walking the streets of a small snow-covered Swiss village. Reading has a magical way of letting you live the moment.

All of these experiences become my living scrapbook. While I may have photographed many such moments and collected those images in real scrapbooks that are stored in my study, most importantly, they are imprinted in my mind's eye, engraved upon my psyche. There they reside, all awaiting that moment when need, desire, and information converge to provide inspiration. What might seem like an instantaneous spark, a spontaneous reaction, a sudden cry of "I've got it!" is really a slow-boiling kettle finally building to a strong, steady whistle.

Elsie de Wolfe's famous pronouncement—"A house should be attractive, comfortable, and suitable. The food should be good; you should be beautifully dressed"—says it all. To elaborate, I might add that the flowers should express your sensibility; the atmosphere should reflect your personality; and the housekeeping should be impeccable. Billy Baldwin, who designed homes for philanthropist Brooke Astor and fashion icon and editor Diana Vreeland, among others, would chime in, "You should be surrounded by things you like, that make you feel comfortable. It's as simple as that."

Breathing vitality into a home, having a zest for life and a flair for living is not something that can be specifically taught. It's not a skill that can be acquired in a classroom. Sometimes I think it's more a quality gained through osmosis, by associating with people who live life full tilt to the wind.

Two people who understood how to "mine" the information that would guide them in their decorating ventures were John Fowler and Nancy Lancaster, one of the greatest decorating partnerships of the twentieth century. Many factors contributed to making their working relationship so successful. What most people remember about this extraordinary duo are the signature schemes, specific houses, or the fabrics that they either created or recreated from various documents. To me, first and foremost among their myriad talents was the unique ability to humanize rooms. The ambience they created with the presence of good books, flowers, fragrance, personal objects, and collections was far more important than the decoration itself; in fact, these elements made the decoration come alive and infused it with an inimitable flair for living. "Living"—again, the operative word.

As an interior designer, it has always been essential for me to ensure that "life after decorating," after the installation, has a secure foundation and a depth of meaning for my clients. Helping them enjoy their homes and make the most of what they have bought and accumulated, guiding them in developing their own personal aesthetics, enhancing their lifestyles, and creating individualized backdrops that aid them as they go about their daily routines—that's designing lives, not just designing houses. None of this could be done successfully without understanding the basic movements, and patterns of a person's life. You must understand what and where people eat, how they dress, what they read, how they entertain, and what they do for amusement, Then and only then can you create a home where all of these activities can be carried out elegantly, comfortably, practically, and confidently.

To create rooms for other people to live in is to undertake an enormous responsibility, one that includes accepting the fact that, in the end, the rooms must reflect the preferences, needs, desires, and dreams of someone else—the client. You must do your homework and get to know the person, the house, the geography. Consider their past and project into their future. And the job also requires maintaining a sense of humor, even in the toughest situations, remaining firm and standing your ground with confidence. That is, after all, why you were hired—for your

expertise, sense of style, and wealth of knowledge, accumulated through years of experience.

Decorating is a psychological and emotional journey of discovery. Sometimes we joke about how it can be as tedious and time-consuming as an archaeological dig. But it's always exciting to start something new, to pique curiosity, to reach beyond your comfort zone and explore fresh territory.

I want to energize, motivate, and inspire my clients to do something fun and creative in their homes. How we decorate and what we collect are embodiments of all that we are—our preferences, our beliefs.

To create beautiful, livable rooms is an acquired skill. When I started my career in interior design, in 1985, that is what I aspired to. Now, years later, I have created many rooms, some beautiful, elegant, and inviting, some comfortable, functional, and practical—and most, a bit of both. Today, my priorities have shifted a little. Beauty is always the driving force, but without joy and delight and the knowledge that living is what truly matters, beautiful rooms are simply volumes of space filled with inanimate objects.

I began this preface with the assertion that living is a luxury. I will end it by explaining why I titled this book *A Flair for Living*—because a flair for living is the ultimate goal. Growing up, I had a mother who swam, dove, cooked, gardened, sewed, knitted, and managed a house with five children—my parental muse. Then there are the spirited women I have grown to love, admire, and emulate—those artists, writers, fashion icons and editors, decorators, and designers of the past whom I have read about and studied, along with many equally gifted women of today, some that I have met and some that I know, who inspire me daily. The silent muse does speak. She speaks to me every day, an inner voice coaxing, prodding, pushing, urging, "Live for today. Today is all there is." Learning how to really live, to cultivate a flair for living in all you do, is a lifelong process. Now doesn't that add a sense of urgency to what you are doing right now? What are you doing right now?

Introduction

What makes a room wonderful is nothing you can see. It's something you feel. You can sense as soon as you enter a room whether someone has been thoughtful. Has he considered where the furniture wants to be? Has she found the most inviting arrangement of chairs in relation to the fireplace or the big bay window? Is there a corner I'm drawn to, where I would love to curl up and read? That's the real test for me. Has someone thought long and hard about how the room will be used and then created just what you need, exactly where you want it? Is the dining room meant mainly for entertaining, or will the family eat here every day? Does the guest room make you long to be invited, and invited back? Good design is all about being thoughtful. It's not just about shopping for furniture and pinning beautiful fabrics up on a scheme board and thinking they look great. Before you start playing with color and pattern, you have to get the architecture right. Then you can figure out the best arrangement of furniture. As you're fitting the pieces together, you have to consider shape and proportion, the balance of color and line. Decorating is about placement and details and the challenge of finding just the right object. If you've been selective, it will show.

In a room that really works, I feel warm, as if I've been wrapped in a blanket. A good room will draw you like a magnet. It will have personality. That's how we're attracted to people. The chemistry is either right or it's not; you're either drawn to someone or not. If a room is warm and inviting, it's because someone has thought about how that room will open its arms and be ready to receive guests, just like a good hostess. The arrangement of furniture should encourage conversation because that interaction is what brings a room to life. There's an energy that reverberates in a room when it's filled with people who want to be there.

Gracious Style

Pagoda for personal stationery adapted from a special volume in my library, Ornamental Architecture by Charles Over, 1758

A Wonderful Time— isn't that the point of it all?

FROM THE LIBRARY OF

CHARLOTTE MOSS

A Wonderful Time
intimate portrait of the good life
by Slim Aarons

Lunch alfresco at home

Madeline Castaing's country
house—in her inimitable style

Your home reflects more than you know. Generosity and kindness are the rugs, hospitality the furniture, curiosity the objects, and originality the placement. Enthusiasm, joy, and vitality make up the fragrance that fills the air. All of these emotions and characteristics are communicated from the moment you open the front door—in the **foyer**. What makes a house work? I think Nancy Lancaster and John Fowler, who perfected in the middle of the last century what we think of as the English country house style, explained it very well. Lancaster, a pioneering twentieth-century tastemaker, famously said that decorating is about the minutia of life. It's not about the provenance of furniture or the architecture or the art. It's about something far simpler. What are the patterns of a client's daily routine? Are they early risers or nocturnal? Do they eat breakfast standing up at a counter or sitting at the dining table? Do they hang or fold their shirts? Do they watch television? Do they love to read? Do they garden? The important questions are, What do they do? And how do they do it? All the little things add up to a much bigger question, which I have to answer for myself if I'm going to successfully decorate a house for my clients: What are their priorities in life? Do they know how to live? If the house is to be the center of their universe, then it has to be tailored to them. If the inside of a house doesn't function well, then the individuals who live in it won't be able to function at their best outside, in the world. Some people look at pictures in a book and say, "But people don't live that way anymore." I say, "Then they're just not living."

16

When you first walk into my house, mirrored French doors separate the vestibule from the foyer. Portieres made from a green damask soften the limestone floor and define the transition to the gallery. You look directly through the gallery across the dining room into the garden. Green is the color you see at the beginning and all the way through to the end. I re-**18** moved the wood floor and replaced it with limestone so there would be one continuous line of stone greeting you at the front door and leading you to the garden. I think of it as a path. Very practical. This is a very active household. I have a husband with golf clubs. We have dogs. Limestone is a strong surface, very forgiving, and I like the way it reflects light. The foyer is the scene of all the comings and goings. It's the last thing I see before I leave in the morning and the first thing I see when I return. As soon as I step inside, I feel a sense of relief and security. It gives me great pleasure to see the big Chinese urns filled with flowering branches, to put my bag down on a beautiful chair. There are feelings associated with all these pieces and rooms. What is important to me is that the rooms I create exude warmth and hospitality. I want them to spell comfort and ease and livability. A room should have atmosphere. It should evoke a mood or stir an emotion and give you something to think about. I want my rooms to be informed. I want them to resonate. I want a room to invite you in, and I want you to accept the invitation to look closer—to touch, to feel the room's sensuality, to wander, and then sit and linger. And then I want you to want to come back again.

A Swedish clock hangs over a marble-topped Italian bookcase in the vestibule. In the gallery, a painted console is flanked by two Chinese Gothic chairs that once belonged to Nancy Lancaster. Every day as I pass her chairs, I feel as if she is putting her hand on my shoulder. I have a palpable sense of her presence, and I'm reminded of the exuberant spirit of this self-taught decorator. Actually, she would have bristled at the term. As she said, "I am not a decorator but a percolator of ideas." What a wonderful phrase. The watercolors on either side of the Georgian giltwood mirror are eighteenth-century French, in the style of artist Hubert Robert. Still in their original frames, they depict pastoral scenes with ruins. I love ruins and fragments. For me, they have a mysterious, evocative quality that can be more beautiful than the complete objet d'art. The wall behind them was painted to look like limestone and was done by James Alan Smith, a brilliant decorative painter, who always seems to know exactly the effect I'm after. I wanted the wall to look natural but not cold, and now it seems all of a piece with the limestone floor. I like the contrast of the dark blue watercolors against the pale faux-stone. The lamps cast a soft light, subdued by the green silk shades. I love the deep rich colors and bold scale of the Chinese bowl and heaped it with baby pineapples, a traditional symbol of hospitality. I want people to feel welcome as soon as they walk into my home.

24 I think it's time to redefine the living room, don't you? To call one room the living room seems odd, because I live in all my rooms. So what to call it? The **drawing room**? That sounds less stuffy if you think of it as a room so beautiful that it draws people in. Formal or informal, it's generally the most public room in the house, where people are received. So you need plenty of seating. The most hospitable piece of furniture one can own is a comfortable chair. For one client, I designed two big, deep-seated easy chairs and then completed the circle with a sofa by Jansen and two straight-backed chairs. You can perch or you can lounge, depending on your mood. In my own drawing room, I have two comfortable chairs flanking the fireplace, a pair of Louis XV chauffeuse that were once owned by Elsie de Wolfe—another of my decorating muses. I'm not sure if Elsie would have covered them in pink, but it certainly gets your attention. For me, the ideal drawing room would be a big room with four corner banquettes, a big coffee table in front of each one, and small chairs that are easy to pull up when the conversation gets going. So you would have these intimate exchanges happening all around the room. It's all about encouraging conversation. And to do that, you have to make people comfortable. It also helps if they look good. Billy Haines, the Hollywood decorator, designed his chairs low to the ground, so every woman would look as if she had long legs, stretched out to the side like a swan or curled up underneath her. In the middle of the room would be a big table full of books and flowers and intriguing objects. I love furniture, objects, and people with histories. History enriches your life and teaches you something. It gives life relevance.

Diana Vreeland once said that she wanted to be drowned in beauty. Nancy Lancaster was always searching for it. I can't remember a time when I was not drawn to beautiful things, and I want to be surrounded by them at home. The black-lacquered chinoiserie secretary in my drawing room is Dutch. There's not a drawer in it that isn't decorated, and each one tells a little story in pictures. It's a novel in black lacquer. The bronze inkstand on a mirror plateau was once owned by the American heiress and philanthropist Doris Duke and so was the chair, a nineteenth-century French hairdressing chair with a dip in the back, caned and covered in leather. I love chairs and I love history; this was a merging of the two. The floor-to-ceiling windows in my drawing room, each with a Juliet balcony, overlook the garden at the back of the house. In front of them is the sofa, which is reminiscent of old Hollywood with that voluptuous curve. It embraces you as you sit, as if its open arms were just waiting for you. There's a small table nearby where a guest can put down a drink. The ottoman is not just for feet. Sometimes there will be four women sitting on it comfortably during a party. It can also hold a tea tray or a stack of books. The bust is French—the brave lawyer Antoine Barnave who literally lost his head after he befriended Marie Antoinette. What he represents to me is courage, conviction, and elegance. He was an antiroyalist who changed his mind once he met the doomed queen and stayed true all the way to the guillotine. I love his strong, handsome silhouette, staring off into the distance.

28

One day I went to Mallett, the distinguished English antiques store on Madison Avenue, to see a chair for a client and walked out with three paintings by the French artist Paul César Helleu for myself. A patron commissioned Helleu to paint four statues at Versailles, but when he finished, he kept the paintings for himself. Three of them are now in my drawing room (the fourth remains with his family). The one to the left of the fireplace portrays the Roman mythological goddess Diana the Huntress, and that's me, always on the hunt for the perfect objet. It hangs over one of a pair of nineteenth-century Italian consoles made of green-painted wood and silver gilt. When I come down the steps from my bedroom in the morning, that glint of gold is the first thing I see. The paint on the walls is a soft strié of beige and pearl gray. From a distance, it looks almost like old wood. The mirror is Chippendale. The tall, pale green chair is a nineteenth-century French tub bergère that really hugs your shoulders, upholstered in green silk. For some reason, men gravitate to that chair. It is the most commanding chair in the room—and very comfortable. There is something extremely pleasant about being able to lean back in a chair and feel completely protected. All the furnishings in this room have a unique shape and personality. It's like a party to which one has invited only the most interesting people. Very eclectic, totally unpredictable, and bound to be stimulating. There's an eccentric little telescoping table next to the sofa that reminds me of a palm tree. The giltwood chandelier is also carved to look like branches. Flora and fauna is clearly a favorite theme of mine. I love all those leaves and paws.

34 Opposites attract. I love the delicacy of a giltwood chair against the bold marquetry of the Louis XVI secretaire. That's husband and wife right there—a big, strong, gutsy piece next to a slender, elegant chair. It's a marriage of furniture. The giltwood side chair is one of a set supposedly made by Georges Jacob for Marie Antoinette. At the Paris Biennale a few years ago, it took a very decisive client all of 30 seconds to make the decision to buy them. Then it took months to extract them from France, due to various permits that had to be acquired because of the chairs' historical significance. Since the original upholstery was long gone, I felt thoroughly justified in recovering them to our taste. I chose a delicately woven silk lampas, the kind of fabric that Louis XVI might have admired on a long gown swishing through the Hall of Mirrors. The seat and back were upholstered using a cushion technique and framed with rope and gimp. It's a style appropriate to the chair, and the upholstery is done just the way it would have been back in the eighteenth century. I might update an antique chair with a modern fabric, but I like to respect the shape and proportions of the original upholstery. It's my way of honoring a period piece.

This drawing room faces west to the Rocky Mountains, so it's filled with light in the afternoon. The walls and sofas are covered in shades of white—ivory, oyster, cream—that take on the color of the setting sun and radiate warmth. The pale rug picks up the glow. Then I brought in more blue and celadon with the fabrics on the chairs. The palette is very soothing, which defers to the strength of the paintings. It also suits the clients' collection of Chinese porcelain. One of the first things you notice is a pair of four-feet-tall eighteenth-century Famille Rose lidded jars with an acid green in the pattern that's very unusual. They're like sentries in the corners, holding court. Another favorite piece is that pale green bombé chinoiserie commode, very feminine and delicate. The detailing on it is exquisite. The marquetry and parquetry on the rest of the furnishings adds a whole other level of pattern and texture to the room. I remember going to Russia and visiting the royal palaces and pavilions of Oranienbaum, just west of St. Petersburg. In one room, the floor was inlaid with morning glories complete with all their tendrils—made out of the thinnest pieces of wood imaginable—curling, trailing. My eye kept getting lost, trying to track the progress of one stem. The custom-made embroidery on the pale green silk faille covering an eighteenth-century French fauteuil has that same lovely, meandering quality. In this room, every time you look at one of the inlaid pieces, you notice something you've never seen before. How wonderful to have that sense of discovery in your own home.

42 Some colors warm you up. Others cool you down. My **library** faces north, and the warm, deep camel on the walls counteracts that cool light. Camel also happens to be one of my favorite shades. It's the color of my vintage vicuña coat. It's the color of old plaster walls in Italy that have absorbed centuries of sun. Then I brought in ocher, chocolate, terra-cotta, and finally sage green, which to me is a kitchen garden. It reminds me of sitting by a swimming pool in the South of France with an infusion of tea, breathing in the pungent scent of rosemary and lavender. I love plants with gray-green leaves—herbs, succulents. They, too, look like they have been bleached by the sun. The color comes in through rich, textured fabrics like velvet, chenille, cashmere, and gaufraged leather. The green silk lampshades are the color of geranium leaves. They soften the light and cast a warm glow, a pleasing backdrop for all the books. This is the room that calls me at the end of the day, to curl up and read. The bookcases are hand-carved with narrow fluted pilasters and built after the eighteenth-century manner, with slots of wood on each side where the shelves slide in. I never have to worry about these shelves sagging under the weight of my books. I also had pullout shelves built into the cases at waist height, so you can take out a book, set it down, and thumb through it in search of a certain reference. I include these shelves in all of the bookcases I build as a matter of convenience and practicality. My library is informed, informal, intimate—exactly how I would want all my rooms to be described.

VOGUE VOGUE VOGUE VOGUE VOGUE VOGUE VOGUE VOGUE VOGUE VOGUE VOGUE VOGUE VOGUE VOGUE VOGUE VOGUE

| MAY – JULY 1947 | MARCH – APRIL 1947 | JANUARY – FEBRUARY 1947 | NOVEMBER – DECEMBER 1946 | SEPTEMBER – OCTOBER 1946 | JUNE – AUGUST 1946 | APRIL – MAY 1946 | JANUARY – MARCH 1946 | NOVEMBER – DECEMBER 1945 | AUGUST – SEPTEMBER 1945 | APRIL – JULY 1945 | AUGUST – SEPTEMBER 1947 | OCTOBER – DECEMBER 1947 | JANUARY – FEBRUARY 1948 | MARCH – MAY 1948 | JUNE – SEPTEMBER 1948 |

VOGUE VOGUE VOGUE VOGUE VOGUE VOGUE VOGUE VOGUE VOGUE VOGUE VOGUE VOGUE VOGUE VOGUE VOGUE VOGUE VOGUE

| AUGUST – SEPTEMBER 1949 | JULY – SEPTEMBER 1951 | APRIL – JUNE 1951 | OCTOBER – DECEMBER 1949 | JANUARY – MARCH 1950 | APRIL – JUNE 1950 | JULY – SEPTEMBER 1950 | OCTOBER – DECEMBER 1950 | JANUARY – MARCH 1951 | OCTOBER – DECEMBER 1951 | JANUARY – MARCH 1952 | APRIL – JULY 1952 | AUGUST – SEPTEMBER 1952 | OCTOBER – DECEMBER 1952 | JANUARY – MARCH 1953 | APRIL – JULY 1953 | AUGUST – SEPTEMBER 1953 |

VOGUE VOGUE VOGUE VOGUE VOGUE VOGUE VOGUE VOGUE VOGUE VOGUE VOGUE VOGUE VOGUE VOGUE VOGUE VOGUE VOGUE VOGUE

| OCTOBER – DECEMBER 1954 | AUGUST – SEPTEMBER 1955 | JANUARY – MARCH 1955 | OCTOBER – DECEMBER 1955 | APRIL – JULY 1955 | JANUARY – MARCH 1956 | APRIL – JULY 1956 | AUGUST – SEPTEMBER 1956 | OCTOBER – DECEMBER 1956 | JANUARY – MARCH 1957 | APRIL – JULY 1957 | AUGUST – SEPTEMBER 1957 | OCTOBER – DECEMBER 1957 | APRIL – JULY 1958 | AUGUST – SEPTEMBER 1958 | JANUARY – MARCH 1958 | OCTOBER – DECEMBER 1958 |

The painting that sits in front of a column of books in my library is by Augustus John, from Jackie Kennedy's collection. Why hang or place a painting right on the shelves? Because I ran out of wall space. Well, it's a bit more than that. The walls in this room are hung with paintings of interiors. This one portrait didn't fit into that theme, but it fit perfectly on one of my bookshelves. Not every picture has to be hung, pinned immobile for all eternity. I use an antique painted Italian music stand to display a painting or two, and I might prop another painting against a stack of books on a small side chair. The casual placement takes the formality out of art and tends to help the room relax. I like my bookshelves to look a little relaxed as well. When books are arranged in elaborate stacks and every stack has an object displayed at the top, I know those books aren't read because it's too much of a hassle to take them down. Contrivances and overstyling make a room look like a stage set or a place people visit but don't live in. We've all seen personal libraries where each book on the shelves is in a shade of brown, green, or covered in parchment—with no titles visible. The criterion on which they were bought was clearly their covers, not their content. How could anyone do that? So many books, so little time. Fresh off the press or dog-eared and worn—it doesn't matter to me. I still love them. I believe bookshelves should be for books. However, once in a while there's a favorite object or collection that needs a home and has a way of migrating to those shelves.

A house is like a scrapbook—an accumulation, layered, autobiographical.

There is a difference between boys and girls, and game rooms have their own aesthetic. Just as much as a man wants to be invited into the bedroom, which is usually more feminine in style, the girls want to be invited into the boy's club. Remember when you were a child and the boys wouldn't let you into the tree fort? This, of course, made it even more attractive to me. This **52 game room** is paneled in antique English oak and centered around a custom-made English oak game table. The chairs at the bar are covered in charcoal-gray horsehair and outlined with pewter nailheads. Because the room is paneled, there are not that many places for warm colors and textures. Hence, the floor is covered in claret-colored leather tiles. They get scratched, they get waxed, and then they get scratched some more. Over time they build up a beautiful patina—like a favorite saddle. These rooms are lived in. Men invite their friends in to play. They are gathering places. In another game room, I had a competition ping-pong table and an English-style billiard table custom-made with compatible bases. Around each table are the traditional tall viewing chairs, upholstered in tufted leather. You want to see each shot and be comfortable as sports segue into conversation. The light fixture, in brass with silk shades, is my version of those I've seen in French houses. I upholstered the walls in a red wool tartan and hung sports photographs. The convex mirror, the largest English Regency mirror I have ever seen, was waiting for me and my client one day on a shopping excursion to Kentshire Galleries in Manhattan. It captures and reflects the entire room—its contents, its inhabitants, its warmth.

Family photos, good music, a warm fire, and comfortable chairs conveniently arranged. Isn't that a simple formula that says home?

Exuberant Entertaining

Place cards from Cassegrain, Paris

Candace

Stained oak shelves and a copper sink were all it took to make a space just for flower arranging

Barry Friedberg,
Chairman of the New York City Ballet,
and
Charlotte Moss

Invite you for cocktails
in honor of
The Aspen Santa Fe Ballet

At home
134 East 71st Street
New York City

Monday, March 7th
6:30 - 8:30 pm

Rhoda Seibert
(212) 407-6702

BURGUNDY
WHITE WINE

U.S. REPRESENTATIVES
FREDERICK
WILDMAN
AND SONS, LTD.
NEW YORK, N.Y.

PRODUCT
OF FRANCE

Mis en bouteilles   à la Propriété

Puligny-Montrachet 1er Cru
CLAVOILLON
APPELLATION PULIGNY MONTRACHET 1er CRU CONTRÔLÉE

ALC. 13.5%   CONTENTS
BY VOLUME   750 ml

DOMAINE LEFLAIVE
PROPRIÉTAIRE A PULIGNY-MONTRACHET (CÔTE-D'OR)

L 04 1

Jasper and sterling
flatware, Rothschild
lilies, citron cloth
by Muriel Grateau,
Paris

Zeze's floral compositions in the entry—what a
way to be greeted each day

There's nothing more relaxing than lunch in the garden on a glorious summer day. The table might start with a bright Indian-print cloth in periwinkle blue, with lots of green and orange and purple. The plates are a combination of antique creamware and new Mikasa. Bamboo flatware is set next to woven cane chargers. I like using antique rummers for wine. A casual lunch like this doesn't require long-stemmed glasses. The water tumblers are simple and clear, from my friend William Yeoward. The **centerpiece** is straight out of the supermarket—or the vegetable garden, if you're lucky enough to have one. Green and purple artichokes, poppy pods, thyme, scented geranium, and basil leaves. I tucked a few silver artichokes in among the real ones, just to throw it off and make it a little more interesting—a vegetable trompe l'oeil. Decorating a table is one of life's basic pleasures. Three meals a day means a lot of decorating practice. Begin with a beautiful set of white china, which will go with everything, and then you can mix in some color and pattern in between. My tables are the result of constant experimentation. I like to play with what I have. Rummaging through my cupboards, I often rediscover something I've forgotten. Even a boring wedding present can come to life, mixed into a centerpiece. Or that gift from your mother-in-law that you don't know quite what to do with, yet it will make your husband happy just to see it on the table. Remember that piece you splurged on? You need to amortize it and I bet it will work on the table—yet another reason to entertain more often.

Just as important as the main rooms in a house, for me, is the breakfast room—the informal area in or near the kitchen, designated for eating. Everyone has slightly different expectations of what it should be. Some want it to feel like a mini-dining room. Others would like it to be a reminder of a favorite brasserie, a Shaker kitchen, or a wicker porch. Whichever mood and style you prefer, the result should be beautiful—and practical. For one

client, I painted the ceiling in a circular domed **breakfast room** overlooking the garden to look like the sky. Morning glories climb up the trompe l'oeil trellis. No matter what the weather is like outside, this family always breakfasts under a blue sky. The curtains are like a garden in bloom and the chairs are covered in a cheerful gingham check. A limestone floor reinforces the indoor-outdoor atmosphere. In my own breakfast room in New York, a corner banquette is perfect for my husband and me, reading *The New York Times* over coffee in the morning with the dogs. It also allows me to cram lots of people in for a quick, spontaneous lunch. The little Swedish extension table is antique, but the French Provincial ladderback chairs are reproductions from a mail order catalog. I've been collecting still lifes of food for years and grouped them against the sunny yellow walls, which really warm up the corner. I love breakfast rooms because they have such a feeling of warmth and intimacy, and I try to make room for them whenever I can. For another client, we set up a dining table in the pantry. Now the family can eat breakfast, lunch, or dinner surrounded by their beautiful things. The room is lined with glass-doored cabinets filled with their china, crystal, and silver. I like the idea of eating in the pantry, and making rooms work overtime by using them in different ways. It gives you the opportunity to play with your space and experience more of your own home. A foyer can be a wonderful space to set up a dining table. I also love to entertain in the library. A dinner doesn't have to take place in the dining room. When you're having people over, don't forget about other possibilities in the rest of the house. Nothing is more fun than a large party, where every room is engaged.

The dining room is the best place I know for entertaining my friends. It is the one room in the house, besides the bedroom, that is used primarily at night. Because of this, we can afford to glam it up. Make it more dramatic. Have fun. After all, isn't that the point of entertaining? A dining room represents a significant portion of what I call the public real estate section of a house. It should be used, not just walked by on the way to someplace else. Is the light great? Then think about reading your newspaper there in the morning or sitting down for a cup of tea in the afternoon. The walls of my dining room are covered in a hand-painted wallpaper by de Gournay in a lovely shade of blue-green, depicting Chinese pots bursting with quince, lemon, lime, and orange trees. I selected the colors and shapes for the pots and then chose specific trees to go in them. Then the artists at de Gournay hand-painted the same pattern for me on silk for the curtains and the organza behind them. It gives you the illusion of seeing through the branches and beyond. This kind of pattern is totally transporting. You are inside, yet you are in the middle of a landscape looking out on another. It completely transforms the dining room, opening it up so you no longer feel confined by the four walls. It extends the garden **66** into the house. In another **dining room,** white paneled wainscoting sets off dark green walls, covered in a striéd silk. I love the contrast of light and dark. Contrast creates drama—a little spark. The silk is an elegant backdrop for the giltwood mirrors, the painted consoles, and the urns filled with volcanic flower arrangements. The table is lined up with the fireplace and centered under the chandelier. Decorating 101, but it really makes a difference. For most people, symmetry is relaxing. Your eyes aren't working so hard if everything is balanced. The consoles are eighteenth-century English, but the mirrors are new. We added some age to them by using antiqued mirror. I have no problem with blending old and new, mixing periods and styles—just like having lawyers and actors for dinner at the same table.

This is the dining room that thoroughly spoiled me. I had the idea of doing hand-painted wallpaper by de Gournay above wainscoting made of Chinese fretwork over mirror. When the clients approved, I was in heaven because I knew how magical it was going to be. The fanciful scene of birds perched on flowering branches and the lustrous shimmer of the mirror gives the room an otherworldly quality. The floor is antique parquet de Versailles, salvaged from a château in France and imbued with the kind of patina it takes decades to create. Venetian chairs are upholstered in a classic Venetian red, and the luxurious curtains are done in a double-faced persimmon silk. From one angle it looks red and from another, orange. I took the backside of the fabric and made a wide band along the edge of the valance and the panels and embroidered it with carnelian beads, in another Chinese lattice pattern. It's like putting a necklace on top of the swags, jabots, and panels. The mirrored fretwork was inspired by a bathroom done by the legendary interior decorator Renzo Mongiardino for Baroness Marie-Hélène de Rothschild, with a bit of designer Tony Duquette's "more is more, and I can't get enough" attitude thrown in. Do something different. Shake it up. It all comes back to that idea of being hospitable to yourself. Get out all those beautiful things you've been saving—for what? for whom?—and put them to use. It would be sad to think that the only time to eat in the dining room is when you have guests. A room develops a patina through use. When it comes to furniture, I believe in equal opportunity. I want all the furniture in my house to have an equal patina. I want all of it to feel adored, loved, and used. That's what makes a happy house, a warm house, a home. When you use your furniture that way, you don't fear it. It's going to get scratched and nicked and chipped, but that's what it's there for. Nothing should be off-limits.

70

It's fascinating to me how you can change the landscape and the mood of a room with a different place setting. Here, we used William Yeoward glasses, silver Elsa Peretti thumbprint tumblers, hurricane candle globes, and tole vases. The Anna Weatherley china brings in a bit of the outdoors with its hand-painted leaves and dragonflies. I love all the rich layering in this room—crystal, silk, mirror, and wood. The dark mahogany dining table is copied from an original made for the Duchess of Windsor by Jansen. I like it because it's baroque without being bulky. The curves of the base offer a nice contrast to the straightedge geometries of the wainscoting. The crystal chandelier and the Venetian giltwood sconces on the wall give off the glow of candlelight, even though they're conveniently electrified. The mantel is antique French, made of bois de rose–colored marble, but the mirror over it is new. The border grid of octagons complements the fretwork encircling the room. The flowers are relaxed and simple and look as if you had just picked them in the garden and brought them in. I love those deep flaming orange dahlias and sent them all the way down the middle of the table in a mixture of vases and baskets. I think everybody at a table should enjoy the flowers. One big formal centerpiece never accomplishes what I want, and it always gets in the way of the people seated in the middle. You can only adapt flowers so much to accommodate that height restriction, which eliminates some varieties altogether. So much for hollyhocks.

72

Setting the table is everyday decorating. For me, it's like making a collage. It's about color, texture and pattern. It's about experimenting with what you have—moving things around and putting them together. Coming up with a brand new combination of plates and linens and silverware you already own is half the fun. I try to mix things up to create a sense of movement and variety. A patterned plate may go on top of a solid-colored plate on top of a textured charger. Layering contributes a sense of richness and depth. Then, every once in a while, you need to pull it back and exercise a little more restraint. After all, the table is not the star. The focus should be on the people and the conversation. I love color. But when it comes to the table, don't forget about white. It's easy. Anybody can put a few sets of white plates together. It's unified and coordinated and this helps some hostesses relax a little more. And with entertaining, a relaxed hostess is the key. White can be formal or informal. I like relaxing my antique creamware with rattan chargers, baskets of mosses and ferns, and handmade place cards. If you're just beginning to collect, I think the best place to start is with simple white china. Build on white dinner plates and white linens. A white Italian tablecloth—antique damask, handed down—is the most elegant backdrop for whatever china you may have. I also love simple linen or printed cotton. And pure white dinner napkins, big 22-inch squares—lapkins, I call them. I've got boxes of them, found at flea markets and antiques shops all over the world. Let everything and everyone else provide the color.

76

Watermelon Gazpacho

Citrus Salad
Tomato Salad with Lime Cilantro Dressing
Mixed Grill with Eastern
North Carolina Style Barbecue Sauce
Sliced Steak, Grilled Shrimp and
Shredded Chicken

Rose Water Sorbet with Chopped Pistachios
served with Cardamon and Orange Fritters
soaked in Rose Water Syrup

Coffee
Green Apple Mint Infusion

PULIGNY-MONTRACHET CLAVOILLON, 2000

CHÂTEAU LYNCH BAGES, 1989

Wednesday, June 20, 2007

As a young girl, I was bit by the china bug thanks to my maternal grandmother, who worked in the china department at Miller & Rhoads department store in Richmond, Virginia, for twenty years. She always had beautiful things, and I was attracted to them. Consequently, all my life I have been picking up four dessert plates here and eight oyster plates there, a stack of beautiful chargers at an antiques shop, and a dinner service for eight bought at auction. I like to mix pieces and play around with alternatives. Different houses naturally inspire various styles of china. For a dinner party in New York, I like to start with a formal pattern from Tiffany & Co. called Cirque Chinois, with Chinese figures on a white background. It's easy to build a table around the bright colors—cobalt blue and marigold and leaf green. I can dress it up or dress it down. It can look very serious with silver goblets and rock-crystal saltcellars and crisp white linen place mats or more playful with citron or kumquat-colored placemats. I bought a large set of blue-and-white transferware from a dealer in Virginia, Kim Faison. It's English, and I love it because there's a little landscape with a pagoda on each plate. It looks at home on top of my French Aptware chargers, with their swirling, marbleized blues. For a dinner in the garden, I might pair it with cobalt blue glasses from William Yeoward and my sandalwood-and-silver flatware. The centerpiece should be easy and informal. I might fill a soup tureen with hydrangeas and march a line of mini-candle globes down the middle of the table. I like the mix of Buccellati silver on a tablecloth made from a sheet (one of the patterns I created for Traditions, called Eleanor). The blue-and-white palette is so refreshing, and it goes with everything. Dining rooms, place settings, hurricane lamps, silver tea services, crystal and chandeliers—it's all about magic. Candlelight reflected in dark wood, beautiful china, exuberant flowers—that's entertaining. Along with great food and drink—and lots of it.

Refined Glamour

Vogue covers copied from
my magazine collection
and framed for a client—
always inspiring

Leave room for spontonaeity, a collection is organic, growing as we discover

CHARLOTTE MOSS
New York

The gray I chose was inspired by Montaldo's, one of my favorite stores growing up in Richmond, Virginia

Chalcedony colored opaline cachepots once owned by Madeline Castaing

Garbo, Hepburn, Swanson, Dietrich—those faces glowed out of the darkness and created an image of glamour that will never fade. Draped in bias-cut silk charmeuse or snappy Adrian suits, they were a generation of career women who set a standard of femininity and shaped a vision of how to look and behave for generations of women to come. We define glamour a little differently today. For me, **glamour** is my maternal grandmother, with a drawer of kid gloves in every color. She had hats in boxes and pocketbooks that matched. She let me play dress-up in her clothes. She wore a fabulous little turban on her head with a halter and a wrap skirt in the summertime. Entering her house, you walked through a sun porch where she grew succulents and orchids. You were immediately hit with the smell of green. The house was full of objets she had collected, none of any tremendous value, but all personal and meaningful to her. The throw on the sofa was handmade. She embroidered her linens and crocheted lace for her pillowcases. She had big bowls of fabulous soaps in her bathroom and let me soak for hours in the bathtub. No matter the time of year, she could go out to the garden or the woods and find something beautiful to put in a vase and make it look fantastic. When everybody else's grandmothers had white wicker on their porches, hers was a rich claret red, with cushions in an exotic, leaf-patterned bark cloth. I grew up thinking red wicker was the norm and white was the anemic alternative. Her house was a place where I was allowed to explore and take part in the cooking and gardening. My questions and my curiosity were indulged. I think that was my first brush with a flair for living. My grandmother did it all. She was a people gatherer, an organizer, a conductor. You knew she was in control, but she was not controlling. You were never anxious in her house. My paternal grandmother wore red lipstick and red nail polish. As she said, "Red nail polish is a commitment." It means you have the responsibility to keep it perfect—no chips allowed. A great sense of humor, so grounded and down-to-earth. She made me practice walking across the room—shoulders back, head high. She always looked wonderful. To me, these two women had real glamour.

Glamour is the photo of Claire McCardell slouching in an oversize bergère. It's the pencil sketch by Rene Bouché of socialite Gloria Guiness in a white shirt, capri pants, and a straw hat—close your eyes, it's so Audrey Hepburn on the Vespa in *Roman Holiday*. It's the elegance of the model Carmen, photographed by Djerzinsky, and how elegant she is today, in her seventies. Who else is on the wall behind my desk? Grace Kelly. Babe Paley. I'm surrounded, and often feel supervised, by some of the great icons of style that inhabit my fifth-floor study. The field is dominated by women and only infiltrated by three men to date—Balenciaga, Man Ray (in a self-portrait), and a small photo of Bouché. The women catch the eye; they are chic and self-possessed. There's Coco Chanel on the left and McCardell on the right, both rethinking the way women should dress, on different sides of the pond. I think glamour is about being genuine, about being true to your personal style, which is not necessarily silk charmeuse and pearls. I've seen a lot of glamorous women in blazers and blue jeans and crisp white shirts. There's always one special twist that makes them stand out, like that pair of earrings you'd never think of wearing with denim. Good grooming and good housekeeping—it's all the same. Glamour is about giving yourself permission to make the bold stroke. Glamour is having the courage to find your inner voice. We live with all these preconceived notions of how we should act and how things should be. Forget them. They create so many constraints and confinements. "Confinement" is a word I dislike, a concept that makes me retreat whether it applies to rules or space. I prefer words like "free," "imaginative," "independent," and "inventive." The heiress Nancy Cunard socialized with musicians and artists in early twentieth-century Paris and changed her name to Emerald because she loved emeralds. The English writer and fashion editor Lesley Blanch, who wrote about intrepid women travelers and was a keen and constant traveler herself, draped her shoulders in paisley shawls because she liked the whiff of the exotic. These women created their own worlds. I have a huge amount of respect for that. It takes a certain type of courage, fierce independence, will, clarity, perseverance, and strength.

MRS. JACK
Balanchine's New Complete Stories of the Great Ballets
Marie Antoinette
Stefan Zweig
The Honest Courtesan
Queen of Fashion

My study. This is my world, created by me and for me. Sitting here, I am surrounded by pattern. The patterns play off of one another and almost become a neutral background, because they have a way of balancing each other out. No one pattern jumps out at you. The colors are duck's-egg blue and pale aquamarine and ivory. The room started with a Braquenié fabric found in a shop in Paris. Big blowsy flowers on the vine—bluebells and peonies and asters—all in shades of aqua and blue. The fabric had been discontinued. I've heard that many times before so I was not discouraged and persuaded them to reprint it. Generally, as reprints go, you need to order quite a bit. So immediately your scheme becomes predominantly one pattern. Then I commissioned my favorite decorative painter and a great friend, James Alan Smith, to create a stencil based on the floral design for the walls but to do it in reverse—with white flowers on a blue background—so the walls and the curtains create a positive and negative effect. The walls of **the study** were painted robin's-egg blue, then crosshatched and **95** stenciled. He sanded the surface to give the appearance of gentle wear and then glazed it, to protect it. When you have worked with someone for a long time, the dialogue can be brief—in fact, James usually completes my sentences. Walls and carpet all play on the palette that started with the blue-and-white fabric. The rug was an archive pattern from Stark Carpet that was recolored in families of warm blue. I have always loved the rich, saturated color palettes associated with Napoleon III, which often include turquoise and red, so as a result there are red touches—a red paisley stripe on a chair and ottoman, red silk lampshades on a pair of turquoise Chinese porcelain lamps. A pair of Italian walnut side chairs, covered in a deep red matelassé, flank the Louis XVI marble mantel and act as a resting spot for more books and drawings. Mercury-mirrored panels inside the window casings double the light and the number of trees I see from my desk.

The other essential is a desk, which goes without saying. Here, I put a desk in a family room to give the client a convenient place to work and make the room even more functional. My own desk and credenza were made for me by Tony Victoria of Frederick P. Victoria & Son. It was based on a blueprint in his vast archive. We lengthened the dimensions and added shelves underneath. I'm a visual person—I cannot have things hidden away in a filing cabinet. Active projects like museum work, fund-raising, and gardening symposia are all around me. There's an easel that currently displays a photograph of Dorian Leigh by Cecil Beaton. I like the flexibility of an easel. It lets me rotate my pictures. I'm always suggesting something similar to my clients. Buy a bookstand to show off a beautiful book, open to a favorite page. Change it from time to time. There are so many great books. Why keep them closed up on a shelf all the time? Drift...dream...as you begin decorating. Dreaming is underrated and underutilized. It has spawned entire industries, great works of art and architecture, magical interiors, fabulous haute couture, and scientific discoveries. Do you need another reason to dream? My study is the place where my ideas gel, where I come to sit early in the morning or work into the wee hours of the night. As the traffic slows down and the street gets quieter, I may open a window to breathe in the air and catch the rustle of leaves. This is how I like to work, surrounded by my books. They give me pleasure just knowing they're there, like old friends. The books are my tools, the decoration is my comfort, and the pictures are my inspiration. I look up at the photos—Colette, Vita Sackville-West, Tina Turner—and one thought sparks another. Someone once asked me what I wanted for Christmas, and I said, "A week in my study with food left by the door, a good supply of red wine, and my dogs." I have everything I need here—I am literally in my own little world. My goal is to have more time to enjoy it. The most personal thing we can do is create a home; the best thing we can do is spend time in it.

99

How we decorate, what
we collect is the embodiment
of all that we are.

Remember those forts you were always building when you were a kid? Perhaps it was a sheet over a card table or a lean-to of branches in the woods. Tree houses, clubhouses, playhouses—they were all about creating your own private space, a little world within the world. For me, as a grown-up, I'm still building forts. No matter how big or small your house is, you still need a little space that's yours. Only now, my fort is a four-poster bed. Sitting in my bed, reading, writing—with books, dogs, coffee and papers within arm's **102** reach—is my idea of bliss. My **bedroom** is the one place I can retreat to and shut out the world. All my other corners—the kitchen, my study, the library—remind me of responsibilities. There is always a list of things waiting to be done. But my bed is sacrosanct. It sits a little higher than average and is encased in and draped with yards of fabric. It's a glamorous refuge— furniture as beguiling as a ball gown. Four-poster beds are innately glamorous, a throwback to the stately beds of the seventeenth and eighteenth centuries, when kings conducted business from their beds. A four-poster has attitude. It's a place to withdraw to and withdraw from whatever you would rather escape, for the moment. My preference for four-poster beds could have developed in part because I love feeling I am in a room within a room. My bed in New York is actually a *Lit à la Polonaise*, with a wood-framed canopy, bed hangings, and a footboard and headboard at the same height. What's the first thing you see when you wake up in the morning? I see a tent of pale pink linen with walls upholstered in a French floral. It's my indoor garden in the middle of the city. Faience pots on the mantel are brimming with clematis, suggesting the lushness of an overgrown garden.

This is big-girl's pink, done for a client who adores the color. It's sophisticated and at the same time it feels playful and fresh, whether it's a deep raspberry or a sporty pink plaid that reminds me of a Chanel suit. The color is an unexpected backdrop for the client's striking collection of black-and-white photography, which offsets some of pink's traditional sweetness and gives it an edge. But what gets the most attention in this room is the bed. I have always been drawn to the idea of a bed floating in the middle of the room. There is no rule that says a bed must be against a wall but we keep putting them there. Why? There is a famous photograph of fashion icon Pauline de Rothschild sitting next to her bed, which is in the middle of her room. The bed breathes; it's not confined. A breeze seems to flows through it, evoking air, light, and freedom—as if you were lying in a hammock strung between two trees. From this position, I can see all around me. It's like living on a magic carpet... Perhaps Pauline's bed was my subliminal reference here. While this bed isn't the same and it is against the wall, it creates a similar impression. When you walk into the room, you look right through the bed to the mirror beyond, and the reflection seems to go on and on. The bed itself, modeled on one I slept in at the Château de Bagnols in France, is crowned with a wooden canopy and draped in a document floral stripe of pink, grey, periwinkle, and citron. Madeleine Castaing, the influential French decorator, loved this print and it's still sold by Clarence House today. Inside, the canopy is lined in a minute pink-and-white silk check. In the old days, a simpler fabric was used inside for economic reasons, just as the French would put a simpler fabric on the back of a chair. But some people like to reverse it and put the fancier fabric inside, where they can see it when they're in bed.

If there is one room that expresses all that you are—your personal style, your favorite things—it's the master bedroom. My client loves blue and loves embroidery, and the embroidery on this headboard, covered in an ottoman-weave silk, is extraordinary. The undulating ribbons and bows are entwined with forget-me-nots, all hand-done by Penn & Fletcher in a luxurious combination of velvet and silk appliqué with velour topstitching. The embroidery on the curtains was also made-to-order. The delicate string of hearts, hand-stitched in ivory on pale blue silk faille, was adapted from a design done in the 1920s by the French designer Armand-Albert Rateau for the couturier Jeanne Lanvin's boudoir. When the client told me how

much she liked blue, I immediately scrolled through my memory to the most beautiful blue rooms I'd ever seen, and Lanvin's was at the top of the list. It was so beautiful, and so restful. A master bedroom, for me, is really about tranquility. It should have some of the same qualities as a great luxury hotel suite. The master bedrooms I design are not just for nighttime. I make sure they can function twenty-four hours a day. There will be a sitting area with a comfortable place to read, a table or desk with a phone. In this room, the pink sofa is near the windows, where there is the most light. Butterflies flutter over a pair of French bergeres, with matching ottoman. The same fabric covers a duvet, folded at the foot of the four-poster bed. Each post is carved with ribbons. Hand-painted flowers and vines outline the feminine curves of the bedside commode. But nothing can quite compete with the tiebacks on the bed hangings. Shaped like bows with Aubusson-style corkscrew tassels, they were handmade in Egypt exactly the way they would have been in the eighteenth century, with silk floss wrapped around a wire frame. It's the perfect Marie Antoinette-esque detail to finish off a very individual room. What can I say? Sweet dreams.

Decorate luxuriously,
live passionately.

The way the French use toile—in profusion—is the way I approach decorating with all sorts of prints. I love the flow, the continuity, and the sense of total immersion. Bedrooms that envelop you create a feeling of warmth and intimacy, and nothing does that better than fabric on the walls. Fabric also does what wallpaper cannot do—it gives you the opportunity to continue the pattern in other places. In one guest room, with twin black-lacquered canopy beds, the floral fabric on the walls is also used for the pillow shams and coverlets. The pattern doesn't end; it just keeps going. In another **guest room** in my house in New **115** York, the layers of fabric read as exotic. I want my guests to feel as if they were a million miles from home. On a buying trip to London, I found a unique nineteenth-century faux-bamboo single bed with a half canopy. Then I covered the walls with a paisley stripe in deep, rich oranges and terra-cottas, with shots of amethyst, marigold, peridot, and citrine. The curtains were done in the same fabric as the walls to create a sense of continuity, even more important in a small room. I selected a companion paisley for the bed and a cotton-warp print for the chair and the ottoman. The antique Venetian desk chair is covered in a cotton-velvet leopard print. Terra-cotta silk for the lampshades blends with the walls and casts a lovely downward light. I found a densely patterned flat-weave rug at Stark Carpet in all those same terra-cottas. We trimmed it and installed it like wall-to-wall carpet to finish off the envelope. The terra-cotta urns in the windows and the bamboo shades all add to the exotic mix. The armoire is Italian decoupage, *arte del povero,* found in Paris when I was combing the streets of the antiques-rich Left Bank. The painting of a woman with her dog was bought at auction in London. She just seemed at home here.

The true spirit of hospitality is about sharing the pleasure that you derive from living with beauty.

Toile, toile everywhere—running between the beams and around the dormers, traveling wherever it has to go to cover the space. The room becomes a total toile environment—so characteristically French. Perfect for a sleeping chamber, with walls suggesting cushiony soundproofing. A bedroom blanketed in toile feels like the ultimate nest. If I'm thinking about using **toile**, I might pull out all of my books on French decoration and textile design, along with my clippings file, and immerse myself. How to adapt life in the château or a Provençal bastide to the needs of a client? How to find just the right toile? Of course, the right toile for me is the Zarafa toile that I designed for Brunschwig & Fils, inspired by an archived document fabric portraying garden architecture and classical buildings with just a few people in the landscape. It's not one of those story toiles with hunted animals on the run or the Spanish Armada sinking—not quite the mood I'm looking for. I prefer the bright, lush bouquets of the Charlotte toile (the name is just a coincidence) by Cowtan & Tout that I used in this guest room. Choosing a strong red toile was a bold stroke. I anchored it with a dark needlepoint rug and then selected furniture—a black-painted table, a fruitwood commode, a gilded French mirror, a bench covered in leopard velvet—that looks as if it all came from different places and landed here at various times. I picked up the bright red in the embroidered bed linens—a piqué coverlet with a scalloped edge trimmed in red, pillow shams embroidered in another shade of red, and a down duvet with the slightest flanged detail at the seam. Every item was carefully and individually chosen, yet they all complement one another. Wrapped in pattern, you relax, your shoulders ease, and your breathing slows—just the goal.

120

Both Nancy Lancaster and Elsie de Wolfe believed that a bathroom should be treated as a room, not just a room to pass through but a room for lingering. It may be the smallest room in the house, but they still felt it should be furnished as a room. If you have the luxury of space, you can add a small chair, pictures, and a table for perfumes, bath salts, and other personal items. A chair in a bathroom says, "Slow down. Have a seat." If you're thinking about just breezing in and out, it makes you stop and think

122 again. I couldn't conceive of a **bathroom** without a tub, and it should always be long enough to stretch out in. This bateau-style antique tub floats in the space and is so deep you could practically take a swim. It's made of porcelain faced in old polished nickel, which has the beauty and the mystery of mercury glass. That surface makes this tub very special, and with my client's permission I copied it for my own bathroom in New York. There, it sits in a tight little alcove so I lined the walls with mercury mirror, to create the illusion of more space. Special brackets each hold a gilt-bronze candlestick, so I can bathe by candlelight. I love the watery reflections in the surrounding mirror. For me, a bubble bath is therapy. It's essential, and helps me wind down at the end of a long day. The floor is made of statuary marble, honed not polished—a simple luxury. My bathroom is more than a room with a bath. It's a refuge, a place to retreat to, the most private room in the house. When I'm soaking in the tub, the world is miles away…Do not enter…Privacy please…*ne pas deranger…*

It's every woman's fantasy—a dressing table, just like in the movies, where she can sit down and get ready for an evening out, trying on various necklaces and pairs of earrings to see what looks best. I grew up with a kidney-shaped dressing table. It had a mirrored top and a skirt my mother made. There were little compartments underneath where I could stash things. It was like having a diary and a safe combined. I never put on makeup at my dressing table. It was for displaying things—a beautiful porcelain bowl my grandmother gave me full of seashells collected at the beach, pictures of family, a jewelry box, of course. And there was always some found object, such as a plant I was nursing back to health, and a notepad—things haven't changed much. I'm still arranging things on my

126 dressing table. There are cuffs, bracelets, and necklaces spilling out of shagreen trays. The color and texture of the stones—coral, cherry quartz, amethyst, aquamarine, tortoiseshell, tiger's eye, and obsidian—delight the eye. All speak volumes for the finishing detail, whether it's a tassel on a pillow or a necklace to accent a certain suit. When I order an evening dress, I'll immediately think about the jewelry that would go with it, or I might select a fabric that complements jewelry I already own. Getting dressed and decorating a room are very similar. Sometimes you start at the beginning—other times you work backwards. If you believe there are no rules, then you are free to do as you please.

Home Couture

Marigolds—who said they are ordinary?

A collector's clock, a rotational airplane and an auction not to be forgotten

Blanc de chine a la Nymphenburg—
(so animated you can feel the energy)

Villa Kerylos, July 2007—
curtain embroidery

Mirrors are marvels of space. They let you see a room twice. They stretch square footage, doubling the space and the light. They can act like another window or dissolve a wall. A mirror at the end of a hall transforms it into a long, elegant gallery. Over a mantel, they become a painting of the entire room. Usually, when you buy a mirror you're not really buying the mirror; you're buying the frame. That's what attracts you. If the mirror inside is as old as the frame, then you have something of special value. Sometimes

I can't find the kind of **mirror** I want, so I'll have it made. For my dining room, I designed a border-glass mirror with five brackets to hold little vases of flowers. How to increase your flower budget? Put them in front of a mirror, or in this case, on the mirror. Sometimes I will set votives on the brackets—more opportunity for candlelight. In a master bedroom with a delicate white Georgian mantel, I wanted a mirror that was equally lighthearted. I found an artist who cuts, shapes, and paints copper, brass, and tole to form amazingly realistic flowers, insects, and leaves (complete with nibbled holes). We arranged the three-dimensional flowers on a simple white frame and hung it over the fireplace. The mirror looks dewy and fresh, as if we had brought a bit of the garden into the room. In another dining room, a mirror with antiqued glass creates quite a different effect. It feels much more mysterious. A mirror has a way of drawing you into what looks like another world, enticing you closer like a great conversationalist. A good mirror is a great investment. Every room can handle one.

Collecting is something I do instinctively. It's like breathing to me. When I see a beautiful object, I want to hold it, understand it, possess it. A collection is about being selective. You are responding to an item for its special qualities. An engraving, a watercolor, a threadbare rug I couldn't resist, a piece of gently worn Sheffield silver with copper peeking through, an opaline vase, a miniature chair—the list of items and objets d'art I have purchased for myself or clients is endless. Curiosity stimulated, energized by the hunt, and satisfied with an acquisition—these are the characteristics of both nascent and experienced collectors. Perhaps it's a flea market that gives you a rush of anticipation, or an auction that produces a thrill when you lift a sweaty palm grasping a paddle. As you become interested in a certain kind of object, you want to know more. Antiques fairs, art exhibitions, and museum shows are all places to broaden your knowledge and refine your eye. At the same time, they help you to narrow your focus. Whatever you buy **136** and wherever you buy it, a **collection** represents you. To achieve the full impact, you must know how to display it to advantage. It is always more powerful to group a collection, rather than scattering it around a room. A staircase hallway in my New York townhouse is hung with eighteenth-century copperplate engravings of various French châteaux—Marly, Chantilly, Versailles. What I love about them is that each presents an incredible vista, with an overview of the building and the gardens and the grounds. They are not the kind of pictures you just pass by. There's actually a lot to see. They are all part of the same series so it makes sense to frame them all the same way. It also creates a lovely unity and a visual quiet in this well-trafficked hall.

**Massing creates composition.
One print is a picture,
seven tell a story.**

I collect pictures that portray rooms. Like a novelette, each one tells a story. They are rooms within a room—in oil on canvas, watercolors, and pen-and-ink drawings. What I like about them is the absent presence, the unseen person whom I imagine in these interiors. Who? What? Where? Cecil Beaton did lovely sketches of his own rooms. I saw some at an exhibition in London and bought them. That's how it started, and then it just grew. Suddenly I was noticing pictures of interiors in auction catalogues, in galleries, and in antiques shops. I particularly like the work of Walter Gay, who painted many European rooms that belonged to his distinguished friends. He was a contemporary of Edith Wharton. One collection tends to breed another. One day, I spotted a little pair of bronze perfume burners with tiny squirrels on top, and then I just started finding more and more of them. I love the look and the warmth of aged bronze and I love fragrance, so the fact that these vessels were used to perfume a room appealed to me. It's a lost art. Craftsmen don't produce them anymore, which make them even more special. The tall Louis XV one in the background was a gift. It stands out amid all the rest, which are arranged in descending order around it. Fine-tune your collection once in a while—play with the placement, upgrade, and edit. If you move objects around, they won't go stale. I am fascinated by the infinite variations within one type of object and love to work out various displays. Sometimes I think I must have been born in a cabinet of curiosities.

142 Like Astrid Lindgren's immortal children's book character Pippi Longstocking, as my niece Charlotte pointed out, I'm a thing-finder. I'm always in search of **objet** that have a future—things with possibilities. I look, I linger, I circle. And then there are those wonderful moments of decorating synchronicity when you know instantly that you want that piece. It's as if it has been sitting there, waiting for you. I first glimpsed this clock in the window of an antiques shop in Paris. It's shaped like a sunflower and I had never seen anything quite like it. The shop was closed, but that didn't stop me. After all, I'm a thing finder. I tracked down the dealer and bought it. I've always thought it would be a great piece to copy. For years, I carried a photo of it around with me, but no one was willing to take on the challenge. Then one day I was talking to Olivier Georges at Lapparra, the extraordinary French silversmiths who make the custom silver I sell in my New York City shop, The Townhouse. When I showed him the picture, his eyes lit up. He said, "You own this clock? Did you know the original is in the State Hermitage Museum in St. Petersburg?" And then he took me over to his bulletin board and there was a picture of the same clock. At that point, we felt that this was meant to be. He recreated the clock for me in the same bronze and gilt bronze. Later I found the candlesticks at an antiques show in Paris and added them to the mantelpiece composition, continuing the flora-and-fauna theme.

There is a general misconception about chinoiserie—it is not always authentically Chinese or even necessarily made in China. Chinoiserie is a European style that arose from a fascination with and an idealization of the Chinese empire. Fanciful lacquered cabinets and screens or architectural fantasies like garden pagodas became de rigueur on English, German, and French soil. Manifestations of all things Chinois started surfacing in the thirteenth century, thanks to Marco Polo. Perhaps the most notable example of its influence occurred in France, at Versailles. The Sun King, Louis XIV, erected the Porcelain Trianon, the first example of chinoiserie architecture in Europe. Its walls were covered in blue-and-white "Chinese-style" ceramic tiles that were actually made in Delft, in the Netherlands. Louis also liked to dress up as a Chinese emperor in full costume—a nod to the importance of chinoiserie at high levels. This, of course, had a trickle-down effect. What **144** the king did, the court copied; **chinoiserie** became the fashionable style. History aside, chinoiserie delights me with its personality, its charm, and its evocative qualities. Every time I travel and discover yet another pagoda in a park or a museum case, I smile. I imagine what it would be like to live in one. In the meantime, I will content myself with a miniature version once owned by Tony Duquette. Chinoiserie is everywhere—from a jacket patterned like a Coromandel screen on the catwalk, to a Chinese fretwork design on a wall-to-wall carpet, to a pagoda toile reinterpreted on paper cocktail napkins. Recently, I found four beautiful lacquered panels in an antiques shop and turned them into closet doors in a guest room.

I want to be transported when I walk into a bedroom. Lushly printed fabrics and intricately detailed chinoiserie suggest exotic places and create a rich narrative.

You never know when a stray memory, an image of something seen on your travels, will rise to the surface. Years ago, on a visit to the Hotel Lambert on the Île St. Louis in Paris, home of Baron Guy de Rothschild and his wife, Baroness **152** Marie-Hélène, I saw a fabulous pair of petite **gueridons** made of wood, gilt bronze, and lapis. They stayed in my head for a long time. When I was designing this house, I decided to create a small alcove across from the dining room, intended for conversation over cocktails or after-dinner coffee. Two velvet settees in a Venetian-inspired design face each other, flanking a black-lacquered chinoiserie commode I found in Paris. What was missing? One might say nothing. But practically speaking, I still needed a place to rest a cocktail or a demitasse. A table of convenience is what was required. So I designed a double-tiered gueridon, collaborating with the atelier of M. E. Dupont, in Paris. It consists of two baskets of gilt bronze, one for the base and one for the upper gallery. In between, the hand-carved stem is made of mahogany. I was still dreaming about that lapis. Unfortunately, the blue would not work with the scheme. Instead, I found a source for solid pieces of nephrite, a green Russian jade, which perfectly complemented the room. Having the opportunity to design a special piece for a special spot for a special client is a great privilege, an act of faith and, in the end, very gratifying. What we are creating in these instances are antiques for posterity.

I like to bring a little fantasy to the powder room. It's the perfect place—small, contained. You can pull out all the stops. And since you're never there for long, you won't get bored with it. Sometimes I'll see a spectacular fabric or wallpaper that would be overpowering in a larger room, but **156** here I can take advantage of it. This **powder room** started with an extraordinary piece of stone—that deep, deep blue granite. It's lapis blue but without any of the irregularities of lapis. It's like having a jewel for your countertop. I combined it with a new parquetry commode made for us in London. The taps, by P. E. Guerin in New York City, resemble gilt bronze and pick up the glint of the eighteenth-century English giltwood mirror. The wallpaper is by de Gournay, hand painted on hyacinth-blue silk. In another bath, I had James Alan Smith paint a faux-bamboo trellis on the walls and entwine it with pink and white morning glories. I found a simple oval border-glass mirror, and flanked it with two nineteenth-century sconces in green tole with little white Meissen-style porcelain flowers. The taps and the faucet are accented with rose quartz, carved to look like a tulip. On a buying trip to Paris, I spotted an extraordinary sink in an antiques shop on the Left Bank and that became the focal point of another bath. It's French, from the 1920s and made of three or four different marbles with an exceptional scrolled base. I took the shape of that lovely curl and worked with another company on the design of the mosaic floor. We incorporated similar marbles and made it look as if it had been there forever. There's a matching marble baseboard and a real chair rail on the walls, but the rest of the moldings are strictly trompe l'oeil. The faux-painting, in an aged celadon green, gives the feeling of boiserie without the heaviness of real wood. It's a very architectural envelope, topped by a barrel-vaulted ceiling.

Every space, no matter the size, is an opportunity for self expression.

Curtains frame a window and define a room. As one of its key elements, they should be meticulously made, generous in volume, and harmonious with the entire scheme. The design of the **curtains** and shades in my New York library is one I have used many times and look forward to using many times more. Straight curtain panels hang on rings behind a swagged valance and a cascading jabot. I am not an upholstered-valance kind of girl. This is the room where I relax and read, settle in for a glass of wine before dinner, and spend hours on the weekend. Hence the need for everything around me to be relaxed and easy, even my curtains. Nothing stiff, always soft, with a beautiful drape. In this case, the dark bullion fringe outlines a little waterfall of Fortuny fabric, lined in the same pattern. The fringe offers enough definition; no need for a contrasting lining. Sometimes the detailing on a curtain looks almost like jewelry. The yellow silk curtains in a master bath are outlined in an intertwining embroidery incorporating pearls at every cross and inside each oval. The walls of the room were covered in the same color of silk and then James Alan Smith painted it with a pattern of bamboo and willow, in shades of white and silver gray. It's a soft tonal landscape that seems as delicate as the curtains. Curtains should not suffocate a room or feel heavy and ponderous. I have never grasped the concept of letting curtains puddle on the floor. Doing what? Collecting dust and requiring constant attention. Like an evening dress, they should move easily, just grazing the floor.

166 Passementerie is all about the infinitesimal nuance. Let's face it. You either love tassels and fringe and use them wherever you can in your rooms, or you don't. For me, it's simple. If it's appropriate for the style of curtain, I use it. Gimps, braids, cords, fringes, and tassels outline and often enhance the shape of a valance, a sofa skirt, or a lampshade. They are the finishing touch that can take an ordinary piece and turn it into something extraordinary. Sometimes you can't explain why a room works but when you break it down, you notice all the tiny details that show someone cares. Details are the period at the end of a sentence. Details are how you take A plus B and create Z. Details are that extra shot of personality. Details are where I have fun. It's the detail part of the project that I can't wait to get to, and it's the details that invite people to walk up and take a closer look. There are the details you create, like those tassels, and then there are the details that you find—what we call decorating serendipity. A screen hand-painted with French chateaus may not be in the best of shape, but if taken apart and reframed, you now have a series of six paintings to hang over a bed in a guest room. Details are inspiring. You want to spend your money on things of lasting value. All that time spent agonizing over the perfect size of a lampshade, the right finish on the hardware, the scale of the crown moldings, the proportion of panels on a door—this is what makes a room—hence a house—really work. All of these design details create beautiful stories that add up to a novel with a happy ending. And a happy ending for a designer is a happy beginning for a client.

I'm always on a visual treasure hunt—for a certain shape of bead on a tassel, a particular twisted thread in a fringe, the perfect combination of colors in an embroidery...

One of the most versatile materials around is ceramic tile. Think of hand-painted Portuguese and Delft tiles or the rustic terra-cotta pavers found in Mexico, Italy, and Greece. Consider the pure white porcelain tiles used in modern architecture or the ancient mosaics that embellish the floors and walls of Italian churches and palazzos. Tile can be colored and shaped to suit the need. It can be a decorative element as well as a key architectural component, covering a tabletop, a fireplace surround, bathroom walls and floors, fountains, swimming pools, and more. Tile can be made out of ceramic, granite, porcelain, marble—even metal. Yet for me, there's no substitute for the cleanness, the clarity, and the freshness of blue-and-white tile. Portuguese, Delft, or French faience—it doesn't matter. The coolness

170 of **tile**, not to mention its practicality, makes it the perfect pool house material. Here, a banquette built into a narrow niche provides a perch for cocktail-party guests. In this case, I used two tiles, one with a light ground for the seat and one with a darker ground to frame the niche. Close your eyes and visualize the reverse, and you'll know this was the proper combination. If I had used darker tiles in the center, it would have dropped like an anchor. Blue-and-white porcelain jars, a cotton dhurrie rug, and large turquoise vases exploding with hydrangea set a tone that says, "Gin and tonic, anyone?"

Acknowledgments

As one would expect, there are many to thank for their contribution to the collective effort that this volume represents—the envelope, please…

To my clients, Leslie & Bobby Lorton, for letting our crew come into their homes for days. Thank you for allowing this intrusion. Luckily with this crew, there were plenty of laughs, too. Most importantly, thank you for giving me the opportunity to help create a beautiful home with you. And thank you for sharing your flair for living.

To Pieter Estersohn, for photography and more—his uncompromising eye, his curiosity and honesty, and the standards that he sets—high! We love that—and for our conversations about travel & places yet to be explored.

To Christine Pittel, for reading my mind, considering every word and crafting a concise and lively text.

To John Bossard, for sharing a vision, his friendship and his passion for the details.

To Jessica Everhart Ludvik, for always believing in the project and organizing all the details from contract to styling.

To Esther Kremer, my editor, the most persuasive editor I've ever had and the guiding light of this project—who never gets ruffled.

To Martine Assouline, for her eagle's eye for detail and art direction.

To Prosper Assouline, for his insights, his ability to see the facts, sift through quickly and make a recommendation that you instantly know will be perfect.

To all the floral designers, who shared their beauty and their eponymous flair for flowers—Zeze and Peggy O'Dea, Helena Lehane, Connie Plaissay at Plaza Flowers, and David & Denise Clark in Denver and Aspen.

For the cover of the book, to Ralph Rucci, for the black gazar evening skirt and so much more.

To Annalu Ponti, for the pair of pearl cuffs she made me years ago.

To Siki on the Palais Royal, for the rock crystal earrings and to Margaret Avery, for hair, makeup, and great girl chats.

To everyone in my household—THANK YOU for holding it all together, preparing breakfast, lunches, cocktails, coordinating Glorious Food, messengers, florists, gardeners, ironing linens, running lastminute errands—whatever it took.

To Sean McNally, for running my house seamlessly, to Wilma & Rosa for knowing just what to do and doing it before we even thought to ask.

To Oscar, for his steady companionship.

To my husband Barry because he believes in, supports, and promotes my efforts, but most of all because he endures…